To Dan

Xmas 1952.

HOW TO DRAW
FARM ANIMALS

TITLES IN THIS SERIES

HOW TO DRAW
FARM ANIMALS

By C. F. Tunnicliffe, A.R.A.

THE STUDIO: LONDON & NEW YORK

First published 1947
Second Impression 1952

Printed in England by Bradford & Dickens,
Drayton House, W.C.1, and published in London
by The Studio Limited, 66 Chandos Place, W.C.2,
and in New York by The Studio Publications Inc.,
432 Fourth Avenue.

CONTENTS

INTRODUCTION

" The Common Boar is, of all other domestic quadrupeds, the most filthy and impure. Its form is clumsy and disgusting and its appetite gluttonous and excessive." Thus wrote Thomas Bewick in his " History of Quadrupeds," below his excellent wood-cut of the despised beast. But that was nearly one hundred and fifty years ago and since Bewick's time many changes have occurred in the breeding and in the appearance of our domestic animals. Gone is his " Black Horse," his " Long Horned or Lancashire breed of cattle " (except for a few remnants) and his old " Tees-water " breed of sheep. To-day, if you were to ask a farmer where you could find a Common Boar he would probably look perplexed and might reply " I dunno about ' Common ' but I *can* tell you where there is a Large White or a Wessex Saddleback or a Tamworth boar." And there you have it : the great majority of our modern domestic animals are of definite breeds which are the result of many years of trial and type selection in the endeavour to evolve an animal which will fulfil a particular purpose, with the result that there are fewer and fewer nondescript beasts to be seen on our farms to-day, their place being taken by animals of specialised breeds.

To-day the farms in Britain are being cultivated more intensively than ever before, and the animals of the farm are inseparable from this great activity.

The Horse is still a useful and valued helper in spite of the great increase in mechanical cultivation, while cattle, sheep, and pigs are all very important members of the farming economy, and their importance will probably increase as farming becomes more balanced and passes from this emergency period of strenuous ploughing and crop-raising to one of stock raising.

It seems then that the grandeur of the Shire Horse, the impressive shape of the Shorthorn Bull and the delicate beauty of the Jersey Cow will, for many years to come, be part of the farming scene, not only for the profit of the Farmer but for the delight of the Artist also.

As you persevere with your drawing of the animals you will inevitably gain some knowledge of farming ways and procedure, and this will be a good thing, for it will increase your understanding of your models. You will soon realise that, in spite of Thomas Bewick's devastating remarks, the Boar is no longer a despised animal. His form is neither clumsy nor disgusting but has a strong virile beauty of its own, and, given the chance, he is a cleanly beast, both in his habits and his feeding. There is no doubt that, if he could return to us, Bewick would see many and great changes in our domestic animals.

MODEL & MODE

The only practical and sure foundation on which to build your representation of farm animals will be the close study of the living creature.

You may at first find it a little difficult to obtain suitable models but if you make a friend of the farmer and his assistants, and do not make a nuisance of yourself by interrupting farm work, your difficulties will disappear. You may indeed find the farmer a willing helper, for he takes a pride in his animals as a rule and may be a little flattered by your desire to draw them. Also he is an expert judge of an animal, and if you can satisfy him with your drawings of them you may, I think, mildly congratulate yourself.

Afterwards, that which remains to be done is to develop your technique and mode of expression, but in this no farmer can help you, for you will be ploughing a lone furrow, slowly evolving an individual method, stimulated perhaps by the study of the achievements of the masters of animal and figure draughtsmanship of all ages. Remember that animal drawing is almost as old as mankind itself and there is a great and varied field to be explored.

I would suggest that in all cases you begin your studies by drawing animals which are at rest. This will give you an opportunity to make complete studies of form and of more detailed drawings than would be possible from the moving animal.

Later on you can attempt studies of movement. These will of necessity be more generalised statements, but your first drawings of form and details will help enormously in your understanding of movement. Whenever possible handle your animal model. There is no better way of understanding shapes and contours than by having a knowledge of that which is just under the skin. It may be bone, muscle, tendon, or fat, but to know just where these occur is absolutely essential; so run your fingers over shoulders, ribs, hips, and joints, until knowledge gained by touching is linked to that acquired by seeing. In time the correct drawing of the contours of your animals will become instinctive.

When drawing from life, a sketch book with a good stiff binding is desirable. Often you will be standing whilst drawing and in the majority of cases you will be in the open air, so a stiff, board-like backing to the pages is essential. Do not forget to include two elastic bands in your equipment. These will prevent the sketch book pages from blowing about while you work. There will often be a breeze.

For drawing I use a H.B. or a hard carbon pencil and sometimes work over this with ink—in my case, brown or black, carried in a fountain pen. But the matter of medium is a very personal one and I suggest you try as many methods as possible from the great variety available until you find the one which suits you best.

And now " to Horse !"

A Shire Stallion.

HORSES

Among the animals, probably none has stimulated the artist more, or been responsible for so many masterpieces, as the Horse. As you search among the works of the ancients you will find him in wonderful Chinese paintings and colour wood-cuts. You will take pleasure in the horses of the Parthenon frieze and in those little horses of the lion hunt in the Assyrian low relief sculpture. Nearer our own time you will discover Durer and his engraving of The Great Horse, and later still our own George Morland and George Stubbs. But the horse we shall be dealing with in this little book will be no fiery war horse or swift race horse, but the strong serviceable draught horse of the farm.

In England the Shire horse is the breed most favoured for heavy work, except in certain of the Eastern counties where a horse called the Suffolk Punch is used. In Scotland a breed known as the Clydesdale is the favourite draught horse.

At one time most farmers kept a more lightly built horse either for riding or for harness work, and on market days they could be seen in their smart gigs and traps, polished wheel spokes glittering, and harness buckles flashing, driving briskly along the country lanes. But alas, nowadays the motor car is more esteemed, and a horse-riding farmer is the exception in most parts of this country, unless he be a follower of the Hunt.

How are we to begin our study of the Horse, bearing in mind that it will not pose to order, but will move often and just when it feels inclined? If you are observant you will soon notice that there are certain times when the horses are quiet or at rest and when quite detailed drawings can be made; for instance, on a hot summer day you will often see a group of horses in the shade of a tree, sleepy and unmoving except for a swish of the tail or a toss of the head. They will sometimes drowse away a whole afternoon in this

A Suffolk Punch.

A Clydesdale.

fashion. At other times you will see the horse in harness probably standing quite still while the cart is being loaded or unloaded—a good opportunity for in spite of the harness there is still plenty of horse to be seen. (It would be no bad thing to make studies of harness also; you are bound to need them later). Try to get the very essence of the animal's shape, remembering that there is nothing so much resembles a horse as a horse.

When you have become familiar with its form you will doubtless want to make some studies of movement, and for these I suggest that at first you follow the horse about the field as it grazes. It would be as well to fix the position of the legs in your drawing and work only when the animal, in its striding, returns to that position. Or again, concentrate on the drawing of one limb, noting the various positions of the stride and the effect they have on the muscles and tendons when the limb is tensed and relaxed. Move round your model

A quick note made in the field.

and draw front and back views as well as side views.

For your studies of more violent movement you must watch your model carefully, long and often, recording your impressions as soon as possible afterwards. Try to set down the movement of the whole horse so that you synchronise front and back legs. This will be difficult at first but " practice makes perfect."

A dappled grey cob. This type is known as " half-legged," that is, neither light nor heavy in build and is used for the less heavy work on the farm.

The drawings on these two pages were made from a big Shire mare as she grazed. She is immensely powerful and a typical draught horse.

16

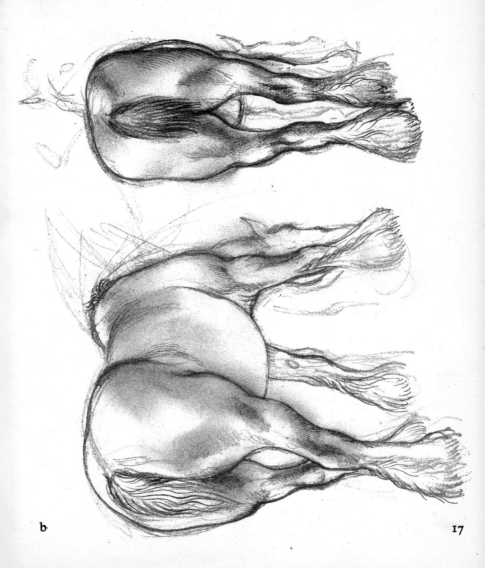

A Shire Mare and her foal. (Note the slope of the hips as she relaxes one hind leg).

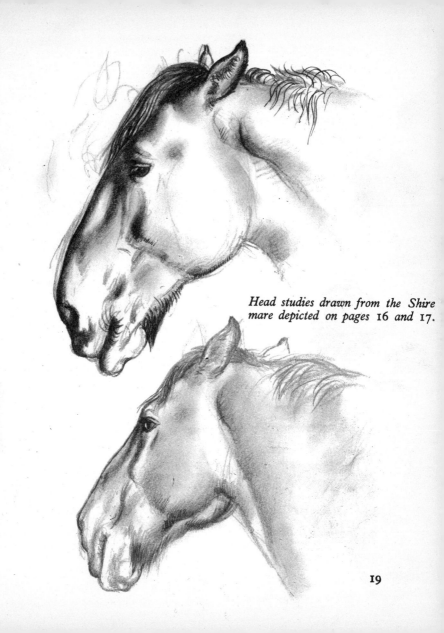

Head studies drawn from the Shire mare depicted on pages 16 and 17.

19

A drawing made in the stable.

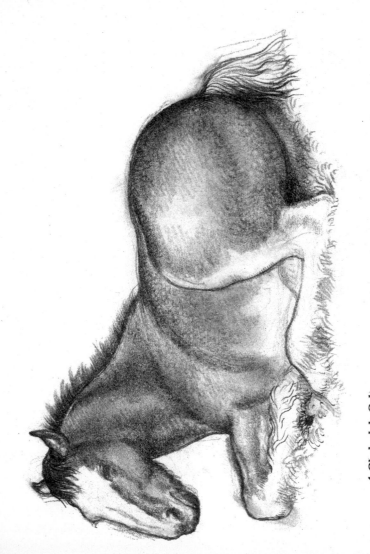

A Clydesdale Colt.

CATTLE

Cattle as a rule are most obliging models : indeed, all you have to do is to sit quietly in the middle of a pasture, where they are feeding, and wait. Soon you will be surrounded by a ring of beasts all filled with a great curiosity towards you. You will be able to draw as many front views as you desire but for other views of cows this method is not entirely satisfactory. However, cattle, like horses, have their quiet periods when they can easily be studied and drawn. When they have finished grazing they will stand, or lie, quite still chewing their cud for a

Shorthorns resting and chewing their cud after a morning's grazing.

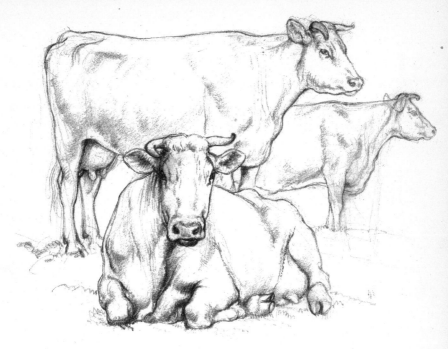

A group of Shorthorns waiting near the yard gate for milking time.

length of time which is amply sufficient to allow detailed studies to be made. Well before milking time they may often be seen by the pasture gate, awaiting the feed of corn which they associate with milking. Often they will stand in interesting groups which I suggest you try to draw Your studies of groups will be most useful when you begin to compose

A Shorthorn Bull. This bull, which was tethered by a chain to a fifty-six pound iron weight, was a very bad model ; it resented the presence of a stranger and gave me an awe-inspiring display of bovine fury. Above is a study of the head made in the intervals between its snorting, pawing, and goring of the ground.

more finished works.

The foregoing suggestions apply to cow models only. As for William the bull, take no risks with him. Do not go into the middle of a field where he is unless you know that he is quiet and good tempered. Even then I doubt if the middle of a field is a fit place to test this. A cattle auction or a market often presents far better opportunities to make studies of bulls. There you will see them tethered in a line and these conditions, besides eliminating any qualms concerning the temper of your models, have the added attraction of variety, for you will rarely find two bulls which are identical. Note how their shape and build differs from that of the cows.

A Shorthorn Bull. Note the powerful neck and shoulders and the lean loins.

We have, in this country, many breeds of cattle and the one you will be most familiar with will depend on the district in which you live. If your home is in Devon you will know the big red cattle with the long horns. If you hail from Herefordshire you will be familiar with the red cattle with the white faces, or if from south-western Scotland the spotted Ayrshire cattle will be first in your mind's eye. But wherever you go in Britain there is one breed which is well known and that breed is the Shorthorn. Because of its general usefulness it is a favourite with farmers, for it gives good quantities of milk, and when its milking days are over it fattens well for beef. For our purpose it is a good " average " sort of beast to draw : neither too big not too small and with a shapely head. If you wish to see many of our breeds together, try to attend a big Agricultural Show where you will find our Shorthorn cheek by jowl with perhaps the Welsh Black or the Aberdeen Angus. There you will be able to compare the smooth delicacy of the Jersey with the hairy bulk of the Highlanders, and the red and white of the Lincoln Red with the black and white of the Belted Galloway. All will display differences of shape and colour which should keep your pencil busy for many hours.

A Shorthorn Cow. Compare the oblong shape of her body with the tapering one of the bull's.

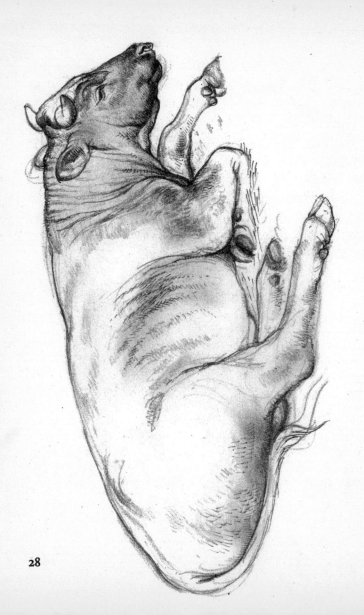

28

This drawing and the one on the next page were made from a very sleepy young Shorthorn Bull as it rested in a loose box. Note the shape of the head, especially the width of the skull between the horns.

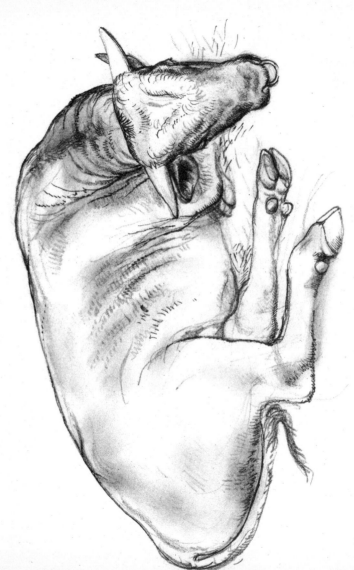

29

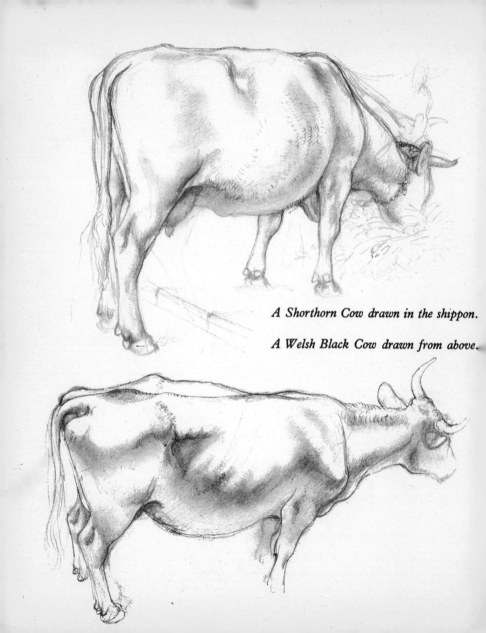

A Shorthorn Cow drawn in the shippon.

A Welsh Black Cow drawn from above.

A young heifer. A Shorthorn-Ayrshire cross.

An Ayrshire Calf.

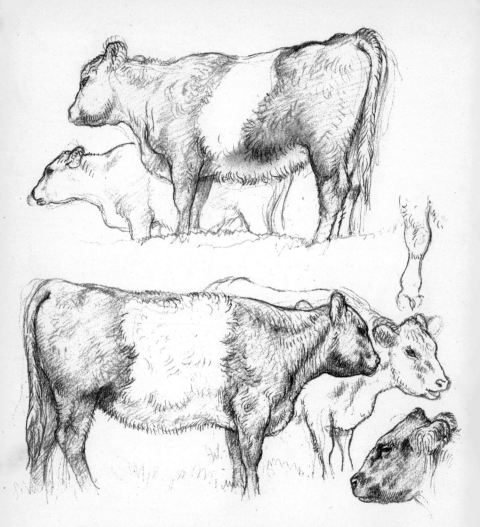

Sketches of Belted Galloways drawn on a wild hillside in North Staffordshire. They are black and white in colour and hornless.

Highland Cattle drawn on the same wild hillside.

A Jersey Cow.

Aberdeen Angus Bullocks.

34

A Hereford Bull.

Ayrshire Cows.

PIGS

Pig, Swine, Hog; how often one hears these words used to describe some objectionable person or thing! A pity: for the pig has not deserved these insults. Most of the objectionable habits which are supposed to be part of the pig's nature have been imposed on it by its connection with man. In the wild state the pig is a clean animal. A dirty pig has usually been made so by neglect and bad housing conditions. True the pig loves to wallow in mud, especially in hot weather, but mud is not necessarily unclean, and certain human beings have been known to do likewise! Therefore, when you begin to draw pigs it would be well to rid yourself of the usual conventional ideas concerning them. Your pig models will be, above all else, very individual, with minds of their own and impulses which do not coincide with the desires of humans. They are rarely completely domesticated and tame, so you will realise that your approach to them should be rather more cautious than was necessary in the case of horses or cattle. Pigs are, by nature, restless creatures, and the only time you may be sure of drawing them line by line is when they are sleeping. Even so you should approach them with care for they are easily startled. When pigs sleep they tend to lie close together—sometimes one on top of the other—and, under these circumstances,

Opposite : Large White gilts (young females).

you will find it easy to make detail studies but rather difficult to make drawings of the complete animal.

You may find that feeding time is more favourable for this, though for the most part our model will have its head lowered in the feeding trough. Again I suggest that you attend the auction, the show, and the market for some of your pig studies, and for the rest there

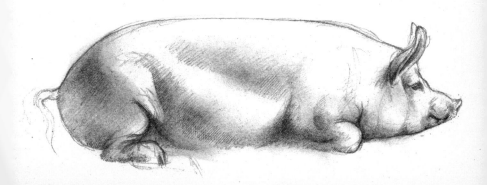

A Large White Boar.

will be many occasions when you can make quick sketches. Be alert, and take advantage of the fortunate moment ; and though your sketches will be, in many instances, the merest fragments, you will be gaining valuable knowledge of your models.

Probably the oldest of our many breeds of pigs is the Tamworth, a neat, alert looking animal of a most beautiful reddish orange colour. It has an almost straight profile from forehead to snout, rather reminiscent of the profile of the wild boar, the ancestor of our domestic pigs.

In marked contrast with the Tamworth, both in colour and shape, is the Wessex Saddleback. This pig is chiefly black, except for a broad area of white which encircles the body in the region of the shoulders, upper ribs, and forelegs. Its build is heavier and not so racey as that of the Tamworth, this heaviness being further emphasised by the drooping ears which fall forward and hide the eyes. Its facial contour is concave, or " dished," as the farmer terms it. Somewhere between these two extremes in pig shapes we have the breed which is probably the big favourite with pig farmers—the Large White Yorkshire. It is a long, shapely animal with upright ears, and will be the breed you see most often. But you will also meet the pug-faced Middle White (which always looks as if it had charged

A Large White gilt.

39

Tamworth gilts.

a too solid obstacle and never quite recovered) and perhaps the pie-
bald or spotted Gloucester Spot and the all-black Large Black. All

Middle White Sow.

Wessex Saddleback Sow and litter.

are interesting and good to draw and I have no doubt that you will become quite fond of pig models.

A sow of the Old Gloucester Spot breed.

42 *Head studies.   Upper, heads of a sow ; lower, of young pigs.*

A page of porkets (young pigs almost ready for killing).

SHEEP

When you begin your study of Sheep you will encounter a problem which did not occur in your drawing of Horses, Cattle and Pigs. In these latter the presence of muscle and bone below the skin was apparent and directly affected the contours. With Sheep, except in the case of newly-shorn animals, this will not be the case. The fleece, even in the short-wooled sheep, hides the anatomy, and when you draw sheep, instead of expressing bony or muscular contours you will be much preoccupied in drawing the masses and folds of wool. From breed to breed the amount, length and texture of the fleece

varies considerably, but in all it will be seen that the wool is arranged in well defined areas. These areas, especially in the short-wooléd sheep, have a close connection with the anatomy (in spite of the fact that they hide so much of it) and are greatly influenced by the flesh contours. The greatest care should be given to the study of the fleece, for your drawings of sheep will not be convincing if you neglect it. It is just as important as the study of the head and limbs.

Take every opportunity to draw the new-shorn sheep. Shearing time comes but once a year, and soon after a sheep is shorn a growth

Left : This drawing and the one above are of Kent sheep, drawn from life as they grazed between the trees of a Kentish cherry orchard.

Kent Sheep.   (the lower sheep is a Kent-Southdown cross breed).

Studies of shorn sheep.   Note the definite arrangement of the wool.

of new wool appears. This means that the length of time available
for drawing the strange, unexpectedly angular shape of " nude " sheep
is very limited and full advantage should be taken of it. During
shearing you will see the sheep in all sorts of positions, many of them
grotesque and very undignified. As a rule sheep remain quiet while
the shears are at work, and this is your grand chance. Unusual views

of legs and feet, the underside of jaws, chest, and belly will present themselves as the shearer turns the sheep and the fleece falls away before the shears—a fine chance to enlarge your knowledge of those parts of sheep anatomy which are normally hidden.

Recently shorn ewes. A Masham ewe with her cross-bred lamb, and, opposite, cross-bred ewes with a predominant strain of Border Leicester. Lamb in the centre.

A well-grown lamb with its shorn mother.

There are also washing and dipping times to remember. On these occasions even the wildest of hill country sheep are rounded up, but both operations are more strenuous than that of shearing. However, the point to remember is, that while the dipping and washing is going on the sheep will be confined in small enclosures, and this gives you and your sketch book a chance to get to work.

Then there is lambing time, but here I beg of you to exercise the greatest care and be the soul of discretion. Always obtain permission of the farmer or the shepherd before you approach ewes that have newly-born lambs or which are near to lambing, whether they be in the lambing yards or out in the open fields. Lambing time is normally full of anxieties for the shepherd. Do not add to them.

About the breeds of sheep volumes could be written, so many and varied are they. Some are short-wooled, others long-wooled. Some have horns, others are hornless. Mountains and fells, rolling downs and lowland pastures : all have their distinctive breeds. On the whole I think my best course will be to draw a few of them so that you may have some idea of the differences in the character and shapes of the " animal with the golden hoof."

More views of sheep belonging to the same flock as those drawn on page 48. Note the " knock-kneed " front legs. These sheep are chewing their cud.

Suffolk Ewes.

A Scotch Blackface Ram.

Lincoln Longwools.

A Hampshire Down Ewe and Lambs.

THE FARMER'S DOG

Long before you reach the gate of the farmyard you will often be met by the farm dog, who will accompany you to the very door of the kitchen, creating a great clamour with shrill barking or fierce growling according to the nature of the beast. Usually these greetings are good tempered and are accompanied by intermittent tail wagging, but sometimes you will meet a dog which raises the hair in a ridge along the spine of its neck and back. Keep your eye on this kind !

A cow dog. A study made while the dog was held.

Another study of the same dog.

If you are in the habit of visiting the same farm often, the dogs will soon come to know you and there will be less barking and more tail-wagging. As they become more friendly your opportunities for drawing them will increase. They will settle down to sleep while you are about, and at other times will not object to being held by someone they know while you make careful studies. But it is their nature to be restless and alert, so do not expect them to oblige with long periods of quietness. Even when asleep they seem to have one eye open and one ear cocked, and the slightest unusual noise will bring them to their feet. Therefore, I think you ought, when drawing the dog, to concentrate on quick notes of poses and shapes, and wait until it is held or chained before doing any very close detailed studies.

55

Studies of a sleeping dog.

Highly trained sheep dogs. Drawings made from memory after a visit to a sheep dog trial.

By selective breeding the farm dog has become the animal we know today—an animal obedient to man and fond of being in his company and within the sound of his voice. He can be amazingly intelligent and faithful, and is, without doubt, one of the best friends man has ever had. Watch him as he rounds up the sheep on some wild fell-side, or as he helps to pen them, sensitive and obedient to every sign from his master. Or again, when at milking time he brings the cattle up from some outlying pasture, note how he nips the heels of the laggards and heads off any beasts which attempt to stray from the road to the farmyard. What would the shepherd and the farmer do without him?

If you go among the mountains of Wales, the Lake District, or Scotland you will notice that the sheep dogs of those districts are all of the Collie breed, and very often black and white in colour. Their intelligence is astounding and their movements are a joy to watch. When working with the flock they never bark, and their tails are carried low as they ripple and flash about the hill-side. They are the essence of speed or discretion, according to the requirements of the moment.

How widely the shape of the dog differs from that of any of the other farm animals! He is carnivorous and therefore a hunter, and these characteristics have moulded his form. Centuries of domestication have not materially changed it, for the padded foot, the thin loins and the fanged jaws are all there, just as they are in the wolves, the ancient ancestors of our dogs.

A trained sheep dog. Its master held it in this position by signs and slight noises until I had made my sketch.

Compared with the Sheep dog, the Cattle dog is more variable in type and colour. Usually there is a predominant strain of Collie in his make-up but other breeds also contribute to it, producing an animal whose behaviour is rather more noisy and unrestrained than is that of the " true blue " Sheep dog. He, the cattle dog, is the one who meets you at the farm gate and makes the great hullaballoo, and he can probably trace a part of his ancestry back to the old Drover's dog or Cur dog. He it was who helped the drovers, when they took their herds from the remote country districts where they had been reared, to the towns ; for it must be remembered that before road and rail trans-

A Corgi Dog. An ancient breed, native of Wales, very intelligent, and used in some parts of that country as a cattle dog.

port were invented this was the only way in which cattle could be moved to the markets and slaughter houses of the towns.

No one knows the true history and lineage of the domestic dog, for in some form or other he has been connected with man since the earliest recorded times.

THE FARMYARD CAT

Where there is grain there are rats and mice, and where there are rats and mice it is fitting to have cats. Farmers are well aware. of this, and often go to some trouble to obtain cats from a strain which has proved its hunting and vermin-destroying qualities. It will not, as a rule, be one of your pampered fireside pets, but a quick, active, strictly useful animal which works for its keep. It will often be lean and half wild. I remember the occasion when one of our cats had kittens in the hay of a disused loft over the pig-sties. She managed to keep the affair absolutely secret until her kittens had become agile and strong. Those kittens never became really tame, and would not approach a

Waiting among the sacks of corn for a mouse. (Farmers seem to have a special liking for tortoiseshell cats).

saucer of milk while we were near. As far as I know they were never handled, but they were wonderful killers of rats and mice, and would spend hours intently watching a mousehole in the shippons or would crouch patiently on the wall of the pig-sty awaiting the appearance of any rat which might venture forth to feed on the remnants of food left by the pigs in the troughs.

Farm cats are nearly always female, the wandering habits of toms not being regarded with favour by the farmer. Your drawings

Cat with a mouse. (A cat usually holds its neck well erect when carrying prey).

Cat and Kittens.

of them will be a case of " catch as catch can." However, not all of
them are wild ; indeed the dairy and the fireside have great attractions
and if the farmer's wife is at all indulgent towards them they become
as tame as other cats, and on bitter winter nights they will no doubt
be found dozing in front of the kitchen fire. For the rest they go
where they will and live a life of their own ; but without one or two of
them the farmyard scene is hardly complete.